OCEANS

Dolphins, sharks, penguins, and more!

Meet 60 cool sea creatures and explore their amazing watery world.

By Johnna Rizzo

Introduction by Sylvia A. Earle

NATIONAL GEOGRAPHIC

WASHINGTON, D.C.

For Alex and Nate—who help me keep the wonder   —J.R.

Acknowledgments

Louise Allcock, Ph.D., Martin Ryan Marine Science Institute
Gisella Caccone, Ph.D., Yale University
Raymond Carthy, Ph.D., Florida Cooperative Fish and Wildlife Research Unit,
    University of Florida
Allen Collins, Ph.D. and Michael Vecchione, Ph.D, National Systematics Laboratory, NOAA
Sylvia A. Earle, National Geographic Explorer-in-Residence
Erin Falcone, Cascadia Research
Chadwick V. Jay, Ph.D., U.S. Geological Survey Alaska Science Center
Karen Jeffries, Monterey Bay Aquarium
Marc O. Lammers, Ph.D., Assistant Researcher, Hawaii Institute of Marine Biology
Chris Langdon, Ph.D. and Su Sponaugle, Ph.D, Rosenstiel School of Marine and
    Atmospheric Science, University of Miami
Eleanor Lee, Boersma Lab, University of Washington
Bruce Mate, Ph.D., Marine Mammal Institute, Oregon State University
Andrew Piercy, Ph.D., Florida Museum of Natural History, University of Florida
Kevin Raskoff, Ph.D., Monterey Peninsula College
Henry Ruhl, Ph.D., National Oceanography Centre
Lisa Schlender, Cascadia Research
Emily Shroyer, Woods Hole Oceanographic Institution
Martin Wikelski, Ph.D., Princeton University
James B. Wood, Ph.D, Director of Education, Aquarium of the Pacific

Front cover: bottlenose dolphins
Back cover: king penguins

Published by the National Geographic Society
1145 17th St. NW
Washington, D.C. 20036-4688

Book design by James Hiscott, Jr.
Text for this book is set in Bembo Standard
Display text is set in English Grotesque

Library of Congress Cataloging-in-Publication Data

Rizzo, Johnna.
    Oceans / by Johnna Rizzo.
        p. cm.
    Includes bibliographical references and index.
    ISBN 978-1-4263-0686-0 (hardcover : alk. paper) -- ISBN 978-1-4263-0724-9 (library
binding : alk. paper)
    1. Ocean. 2. Marine biology. I. Title.
    GC21.R545 2010
    551.46--dc22
                            2009049630

Printed in USA

10/WOR/1

false clown anemonefish

CONTENTS

sea lion in a school of salema fish

BY DEEP-SEA EXPLORER SYLVIA A. EARLE

INTRODUCTION

IMAGINE WHAT IT MUST BE LIKE to be a dolphin, living in a realm of liquid space, listening to the whistles and clicks of nearby family members. Have you ever wondered what it's like to be a jellyfish, with 99 percent of your body made of water? Or how about a clam, hunkered down in a soft, sandy bottom, sipping plankton-filled water through a special tube, rather like drinking soup through a straw? Imagine living in the deep sea, beyond the reach of the sun's rays, lighting your way with the flash, sparkle, and glow emitted from your own body.

As a marine biologist and undersea explorer, I have spent thousands of hours in the ocean, getting to know some of the millions of kinds of plants, animals, and other life-forms that live there—far more than exist on the land.

It is obvious why all of these creatures need the ocean. It's their home! But what about us? We now know that the ocean gives Earth an oxygen-rich atmosphere that makes it possible for land animals (including us) to live. It steadies the temperature, drives climate and weather, and yields fresh water to the sky that returns to the land and sea as rain, sleet, and snow. There can be water without life, but nowhere is there life without water, and 97 percent of Earth's water is in the ocean.

Like life in the sea, we need the ocean, and now the ocean needs us. Pollution, overfishing, and other things people have done to the sea are causing problems that dolphins, jellyfish, and clams can't solve. The good news is that humans can, and it starts with understanding the nature of the ocean—and knowing why it matters. This book is a wonderful place to begin.

Earle greets Sandy, a wild dolphin in the Bahamas.

ARCTIC OCEAN

ASIA

NORTH AMERICA

PACIFIC

ATLANTIC

Mid-Atlantic Ridge

Challenger Deep
-35,827 feet
-10,920 meters
*World's greatest
ocean depth*

Puerto Rico Trench
-28,232 feet
-8,605 meters
*Atlantic Ocean's
deepest point*

SOUTH
AMERICA

Java Trench
-23,376 feet
-7,125 meters
*Indian Ocean's
deepest point*

AUSTRALIA

OCEAN

INDIAN

OCEAN

Mid-Atlantic Ridge

ANTARCTICA

olloy Hole
3,599 feet
69 meters
c Ocean's
est point

EUROPE

ASIA

AFRICA

O
C
E
A
N

INDIAN

OCEAN

0   4,000 Miles

0   5,000 Kilometers

ANTARCTICA

Oceans **of the World**

Pacific

The biggest ocean on Earth, the Pacific hugs the planet nearly halfway around and contains almost half its ocean water. Stretching along the west coast of North and South America all the way to the east coast of Asia, the Pacific contains some 25,000 islands. It is also home to Challenger Deep—the deepest place on Earth and the lowest point in the cavernous Mariana Trench.

Atlantic

The saltiest ocean of all, the Atlantic stretches from the east coast of North and South America to the west coast of Europe and Africa. In the frigid northern part, near Greenland, five-story-tall icebergs loom. Deep below the surface about halfway between Europe and the Americas, lies the Mid-Atlantic Ridge, the longest mountain range on Earth. It's as long as the Andes, Rockies, and the Himalayas combined.

Indian

Formed more than 65 million years ago when present-day Africa separated from Antarctica, India, and Australia, this is the youngest of all the oceans. It curves around the southern coast of Asia and stretches from the east coast of Africa to the west coast of Australia. Powerful winds, called monsoons, blow from the southwest between May and October, and from the northeast between November and April.

Arctic

Wrapped around the North Pole, the Arctic is the coldest of the oceans. It is so far north that the sun barely rises for much of the winter. Pack ice drifts in frigid currents, colliding and refreezing—creating a partial ice cover that can be more than a hundred feet thick in some places. For a few months in the summer, the sun shines almost 24 hours a day, melting some of the ice. Also the smallest and shallowest ocean, the Arctic is almost completely closed off by the northern borders of North America, Europe, and Asia.

A Fifth Ocean?

The Atlantic, Indian, and Pacific Oceans meet up around the continent of Antarctica. Some experts call this the Antarctic, Austral, or Southern Ocean. But is it really a separate ocean? Some say no, that it's just a place where three oceans meet. Others say yes, because the water has distinct currents and temperatures.

Humpback whales are **natural** acrobats.

WHA

LES

THE OCEAN WATER PARTS as two blowholes split the surface, blasting a gigantic spray into the air. A humpback whale leaps out of the ocean belly-up and then arches its back as it plunges headfirst under the waves. This impressive leap, called breaching, lasts only a few seconds, before the graceful giant vanishes again into the deep.

But humpbacks don't just come to the surface to do gymnastics. All whales are mammals that must surface regularly to breathe in air through their blowholes. They also give birth to live young and nurse their babies. Blue whales, the most gigantic creatures known to live on the planet, have the largest babies on Earth. These not-so-little ones weigh in at some six thousand pounds (2,721 kg) and gain about nine pounds (4 kg) every hour by drinking their mothers' fatty milk. Over time these baby blues will grow to be as long as two school buses.

A blue whale's underwater call is as loud as a jet engine, but the tone is too low for humans to hear. Of all whales, humpbacks have some of the longest and most varied songs, crooning for up to 15 minutes at a time. What these songs mean is one of the great mysteries of the sea. Only male humpbacks and blue whales are known to sing, but many species have calls, ranging from barks to chirps to moans, screams, and pops. Some scientists think the songs attract females, or just announce to other males, "I'm here."

humpback whales breaching

GIANTS OF THE SEA

Whales come in many different shapes and sizes. Dive into some fascinating facts about some of these mammoth mammals.

beluga

BELUGA
Length: 10 to 15 feet (3 to 5 m)
Weird but True: It uses its dorsal (back) ridge to punch breathing holes in Arctic ice.

MINKE WHALE
Length: 26 to 33 feet (8 to 10 m)
Weird but True: Curious minkes sometimes swim alongside ships.

NARWHAL
Length: 13 to 15 feet (4 to 5 m)
Weird but True: The male has a giant tooth on its head.

BLUE WHALE
Length: 75 to 100 feet (22 to 30 m)
Weird but True: They weigh up to 200,000 pounds (99,800 kg).

SPERM WHALE
Length: 36 to 59 feet (11 to 18 m)
Weird but True: It can dive to 3,300 feet (1,006 m), deeper than any other large whale.

RIGHT WHALE
Length: 35 to 55 feet (11 to 17 m)
Weird but True: Its huge head can take up a third of its length.

BOWHEAD WHALE
Length: 38 to 50 feet (11 to 15 m)
Weird but True: Bowhead whales swim under the ice when frightened.

Underwater Feast

ITTY-BITTY CRUSTACEANS CALLED KRILL (right) swim in large clusters that provide a hearty meal for giants, such as blue whales, right whales, humpbacks, and others. Unlike belugas and other toothed whales, which eat larger sea creatures, these whales are toothless filter feeders. With mouths open wide, they take in gallons of water along with the thousands of tiny krill floating in it. The whale's tongue pushes the water out, but the krill are held prisoner in its mouth by rows of stiff plates called baleen. Then, GULP, it's a krill supper!

narwhal

blue whale

minke whale

right whale

sperm whale

bowhead whale

JELLYFISH

SEE-THROUGH, SQUISHY, and mostly blind, jellyfish bob along with the rhythm of the waves and currents. Tiny, venomous cells on endlessly flapping and flowing tentacles stun shrimp, fish, and other small sea creatures that have the misfortune to swim across a jelly's path. Without digestive tracts, these blobby creatures use their stomach juices to liquefy prey.

It's not an insult to say a jelly is brainless. These gelatinous creatures really don't have brains. A jelly actually isn't even a fish; it's a drifting animal that can move up and down, but has little control over where it floats sideways. Emerging from its egg, a young jellyfish soon becomes a polyp, or a little mouthlike shape, facing up in the air surrounded by tiny tentacles. The polyp attaches to just about anything, such as a rock or coral. Eventually it turns into a tiny jellyfish called an ephyra, with an umbrella-shaped body and swinging, swaying tentacles. The ephyra is only about a millimeter wide, but most young jellies will chow down on plankton almost nonstop until they become adult jellyfish, called medusas.

While jellyfish stings can be deadly to some sea creatures, for others, such as sea turtles and some fish, jellies make a wonderful, wiggly meal.

Jumbo Jellyfish

GROWING FROM THE length of a grain of rice to the size of a washing machine in just six months, Nomura's jellyfish (left) are some of the largest jellies in the world. Found along the coasts of China and North and South Korea, each giant jelly weighs some 450 pounds (204 kg) and has about 60 tentacled arms that are covered with stingers. A passing fish strays too close. Then it's sting, stun—and dinner! Nomura's jellyfish can also sting humans, but the pain usually wears off quickly. Luckily this jelly's giant size doesn't mean it has a giant sting, too.

Jellyfish use
their **tentacles**
to **drag** prey
toward their bodies.

jellyfish preying on a
man-of-war fish

Sea otters have up to a **million** hairs on every **inch** of skin— the **densest** fur of any animal.

sea otters in Alaska

SEA OTTERS

FLOATING BELLY-UP, backs cradled in the ocean water, sea otters don't even flip over to eat. Instead—CRUNCH!—they use rocks to crush clamshells and to open up spiky creatures called sea urchins.

Using their tummies as tables while they snack, sea otters wash their bellies after every meal so food doesn't get stuck in their extra-thick fur. Whether the otters live in mild or freezing climates, the fur keeps them warm and also helps them float by trapping air inside the strands. After diving under the waves, a sea otter blows air back into its fur, and sometimes it does somersaults as it forces air inside.

This thick fur also helps new-born sea otters bob along on the water with their mothers. But mama otters most often carry their babies on their tummies and even nurse them as they float along with their furry backs facing downward into the sea.

In a behavior called rafting, sea otters sometimes gather in groups to socialize, to rest, and to watch out for each other. If a sea otter outside of the group perks up, the other sea otters suddenly pay attention, too. When orcas and other predators, such as eagles, sea lions, or sharks, are nearby, the otters scatter into the water, hoping to dart away to safety.

Underwater Forest

IN THE COOL COASTAL WATERS of the North Pacific, off the coast of places such as California and Alaska, sea otters often make their homes in forests of kelp, a type of seaweed (bottom right). By wrapping themselves and their babies in kelp (above right) that floats on the water's surface, the animals anchor themselves so they can snooze without drifting out to sea. These giant, swaying forests grow in cool coastal waters, reaching up to 200 feet tall (60 m)—the height of a 20-story building! The plants' rootlike holdfasts grip the ocean floor, while gas-filled pockets, called bladders, keep kelp upright as it stretches toward the sunlight. Thousands of other animals rely on kelp forests, too. Sponges, sea urchins, seals, and even orcas hide, hunt, and eat in the towering leaves and stalks.

Size: 4 inches to 30 feet wide (10 cm to 9 m)

RAYS

A RAY SWIMS WITH A RHYTHMIC

rise and fall of its side fins, almost like a bird flapping its wings. A few up-and-down movements are enough to keep its diamond-shaped body gliding through the ocean. Rays look weightless in the water, but the biggest species, the 2,000-pound (907 kg) manta ray, actually weighs about as much as a cow. As it moves, gill slits on its underbelly absorb life-giving oxygen from the water. It often rests on the ocean floor, safely camouflaged like a rock in the sand, and comes out when it's time to hunt for a seafood dinner.

Rays are gentle creatures, munching mostly on shellfish, small fish, and in some cases, plankton. But when provoked, some rays, called stingrays, use their whiplike tails as powerful weapons of self-defense. With lightning speed, a ray can lash an attacker with saw-edged, stinging spines on its tail, inflicting serious pain.

Electric rays have real *shock* value. When hungry or threatened, two kidney-shaped electric organs in their bodies send out jolts of up to 200 volts—enough to power a hair dryer, kill prey, and keep hungry sharks and orcas away.

Feeding Frenzy

A PERFECT FEAST FOR HUNGRY manta rays lies in Hanifaru Bay, Maldives, a cluster of islands in the Indian Ocean. Plankton and krill pack closely together, swimming in masses that make for easy pickings. First a few mantas arrive, and then suddenly there are hundreds. Mouths open, round and gaping (inset), a group of mantas swims through the tasty plankton in an orderly line, called chain feeding. When 50 or more mantas start chain feeding, something amazing happens. The head of the line catches up with the end, and the rays swirl around and around, creating a manta cyclone. When more than a hundred mantas join the group, the spiral breaks apart. A free-for-all begins, rays bumping into each other as they wolf down their plankton picnic.

manta ray

Some **scientists**
consider rays
flat sharks.

A sea horse
never stops
moving its **fins.**

pygmy sea horse in coral

SEA HORSES

FLUTTERING 35 TIMES EACH SECOND, small fins on a sea horse's back propel the tiny animal upright through the water. Two tiny fins on its head help steer as its curled tail unfurls and trails behind. Always on the lookout for predators, a sea horse can move its eyes in opposite directions at the same time.

To stay in one place, these candy-colored creatures use their tails to grab onto sea grass or coral. These ravenous carnivores have to eat almost constantly to stay alive, gulping up to 3,000 tiny brine shrimp every day, as well as other small animals and plankton. Their long snouts suck up these tasty treats as they drift by.

Sea horses are among only a few animal species on Earth in which the male carries the young before birth. After males and females lock their tails in a romantic dance that can last for several hours, the female sea horse places a hundred or more eggs in a pouch on the male's belly. The male fertilizes the eggs and carries them around in his pouch. About a month later, the father sea horse opens the pouch and gently pushes out the miniature sea horses. The young fend for themselves from the first moment they are born.

A sea horse's closest relative is the leafy-limbed sea dragon. Here's the secret to telling these look-alikes apart.

SEA HORSE VS. SEA DRAGON

SEA HORSE	SEA DRAGON
swim vertically	swim horizontally
can grab objects with their tails	tails are not used as anchors
eggs are kept in the male's pouch	eggs are attached to the male's tail
no fleshy appendages	have fleshy appendages for camouflage

Penguins can swim **nine times** faster than they can **waddle.**

PENGUINS

NUDGE, NUDGE, ROLL—a mother emperor penguin gently pushes her egg to the father. He pushes the fragile cargo quickly onto his feet and wedges it under his warm body. One false move and the egg will roll onto the ice, freezing the chick in seconds. The female then joins a parade of mother penguins on a 50-mile (80-km) trek back to the ocean. But the males will stay on the ice for about 65 days, guarding their eggs and pressing together for warmth. A layer of air trapped under their feathers will help protect them against the brutal Antarctic winter.

Warmer weather finally returns, and fuzzy chicks peck their way out of the eggs. Just in time, the females return to feed the hungry little ones. The male emperors then begin their long journey back to the sea. Penguins can't fly, so instead they waddle and slide on their bellies across the ice to reach the ocean.

When they finally plunge into the water, they become like torpedoes, zooming up to 10 miles (16 km) an hour to capture fish and squid— their first food in more than two months—and dodging predators such as seals and orcas. When they've eaten their fill, they climb back out and begin the extend-ed waddle back across the ice to return to their chicks once again.

emperor penguins with chicks (both pictures)

WACKY WAYS OF PENGUINS

Spiky feathers, striped faces, yellow chests—their funny "costumes" aren't the only surprising things about these penguins.

ADÉLIE
Height: about 2 feet (60 cm)
Weird but True: They sometimes swipe stones from their neighbors' nests to line their own nests. The Adélie at right is jumping off a ledge.

GENTOO
Height: 2 to 2 ½ feet (60 to 76 cm)
Weird but True: Gentoos have long, stiff tail feathers that stick out behind them when they walk.

CHINSTRAP
Height: 2 to 2 ½ feet (60 to 76 cm)
Weird but True: Chinstrap penguins can dive more than a hundred feet under the water.

ROCKHOPPER
Height: about 2 feet (60 cm)
Weird but True: Rockhoppers are known for their crazy hairdos and for jumping from rock to rock.

KING
Height: about 3 feet (91 cm)
Weird but True: Kings are the second largest penguins after emperors.

chinstraps

Adélie

rockhopper

gentoo

Ancient Icebergs

WHEN ANTARCTIC PENGUINS need a break from fishing, they often chill out on giant, floating chunks of ice called icebergs (below). These frozen mounds start out as parts of glaciers—massive formations of compressed ice and snow that can be hundreds of thousands of years old. When the edge of one of these slow-moving rivers of ice hits the ocean, it unleashes thunderous groans and rumbles that can be heard miles away. Then chunks of ice, some 16 stories tall, plunge into the sea. Icebergs are born!

25

A **newborn** octopus is the **size** of a **pea.**

reef octopus

OCTOPUSES

A SINGLE EYE RISES out of the sandy ocean floor. Danger is lurking nearby. The octopus ducks under the sand again. A second look a few minutes later finds that the coast is clear, so eight arms free themselves from the grainy bottom.

Slinking, lurking, watching—octopuses are underwater spies, always on the lookout for a crab or lobster to devour or predators to avoid, such as large fish and sharks.

When they do spot attackers, they protect themselves with escape tactics worthy of a secret agent. Their skin is filled with chromataphores—groups of special cells filled with different colors—which spread out and turn the octopus's skin the same color as its surroundings. The sly creature then becomes virtually invisible as it skirts rocks and crevices.

An octopus crawls slowly while hunting, but when it becomes the hunted, look out! The octopus performs the ultimate vanishing act. Shooting out a cloud of black ink, the animal confuses its stalker. At the same time, the octopus squirts water from deep inside its body. Streamlined, with eight legs out straight behind it, the octopus uses jet propulsion to dart away and make a speedy escape.

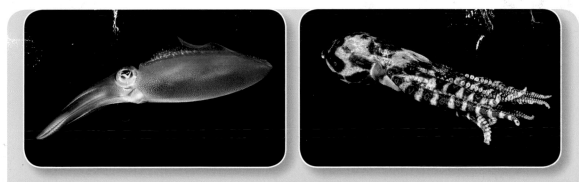

Squid and octopuses belong to a group of marine animals called cephalopods. But these cousins have their differences.

SQUID vs. OCTOPUS

SQUID	OCTOPUS
most have eight arms and two tentacles	most have eight arms and no tentacles
generally lay their eggs and leave them	generally protect their eggs until they hatch
have hooks or rings on their suckers	have only suckers

OCEAN Extremes

WILD WONDERS

The Earth's crust, or hard surface, is separated into colossal sections called tectonic plates, which are in constant motion, bumping and scraping against each other. Volcanic eruptions and mountain and crevice creations are some of the extreme results of all the commotion in the ocean.

Biggest Explosions

Thousands of active volcanoes are percolating under the sea. When they blow, they sometimes spew steam, smoke, lava, gas, and ash hundreds of feet into the air. If an underwater volcano erupts again and again over millions of years, hardened lava collects and forms new islands. The U.S. state of Hawaii is actually a volcanic island chain.

Hottest Habitats

Deep below the ocean's surface, frigid seawater seeps into cracks in the seafloor, trickling into Earth's crust. There, the heat from molten rock, called magma, heats the liquid until a boiling, black mixture of water and minerals burps back out, creating a hydrothermal vent that reaches up to 752°F (400°C). Over time, the minerals collect and form tall structures called chimneys that attract strange sea creatures, such as six-foot-tall tube worms and blind shrimp!

hydrothermal vent

Hawaii Volcanoes National Park

Longest Mountain Range

You can't hike to the top of these peaks—they're a mile under the sea! The world's longest mountain range, called the Mid-Atlantic Ridge, stretches some 6,214 miles (10,000 km) down the middle of the Atlantic Ocean—more than twice the distance from Washington, D.C., to Los Angeles, California.

Mid-Atlantic Ridge above sea level in Thingvellir, Iceland

Deepest Trench

Some of the oceans' deepest, darkest secrets lie in a -35,827-foot (-10,972 m) abyss called Challenger Deep, which lies at the bottom of the Mariana Trench (big picture). Located smack in the center of the Pacific Ocean, only two people have journeyed to the deepest place on Earth. What's down there in the inky blackness is still one of the world's biggest mysteries.

-35,827 feet (-10,972 m)

A stack of 25 Empire State Buildings (right) could fit inside the Mariana Trench.

ILLUSTRATION NOT TO SCALE

Coral reefs
can be **thousands**
of years old.

coral reef in Indonesia

sea anemones

jawfish

French grunts

Largest
Coral Reef
in the World

AUSTRALIA'S GREAT BARRIER reef (above) stretches some 1,250 miles (2,000 km) and is one of the largest natural structures on Earth. Longer than the Great Wall of China, it can even be seen from space!

More than six hundred islands and thousands of smaller coral reefs link up like a massive chain, running parallel to Australia's northeast shoreline. In this sun-drenched part of the ocean, it's possible to see as far as 100 feet (30 m) down into the brilliant blue water. The sun's rays create a welcoming home for at least 300 species of hard coral, 4,000 species of mollusks, and 1,500 kinds of fish that swim and shimmy throughout the reef.

sea cucumber

sea snail

SEA TURTLES

HEAVING HERSELF FROM THE SURF, a mama green sea turtle grunts as she slides her 350-pound (159-kg) body across the sandy beach. She has come home to nest after more than two years away, perhaps traveling thousands of miles to return to the beach where she was born. No one knows exactly how she finds her way, but she may rely on Earth's magnetic fields for her finely tuned sense of direction.

Finding a spot on the beach, she scoops out a hole with her rear flippers, laying 80 to 150 eggs and then covering her nest with sand. She'll return to the same beach about every two weeks for the next few months, and repeat the same ritual. At the end of the season, when her nesting duties are done, she shuffles back to the sea. She doesn't look back even once.

About two months later, baby sea turtles (inset) nose their way out of their eggs, digging for a whole day to reach the sand's surface. The babies' flippers quickly grip, push, grip, push as they race to the sea. About three inches from flipper to flipper, the tiny hatchlings might have to outrun crabs, raccoons, and birds that see them as bite-size snacks. Traveling at night, only half of the hatchlings will make it to the water, just dozens of feet away. No time to rest. Grip, push, grip, push, grip, push…

March to the Sea

ONLY ONE of every thousand eggs laid by female sea turtles will survive to become an adult sea turtle. Here's why:

1,000 eggs are laid, buried on sandy beaches.

800 sea turtles hatch. The rest never fully develop.

400 make it off the beach into the open ocean. Others are eaten by crabs, birds, and fish.

200 survive two to five years at sea. The rest are eaten by predators or get caught in fishing gear.

I lives to be 30 to 70 years old. The remaining sea turtles fall victim to sharks, capture, and disease.

green sea turtle
with yellow tangs and
goldring surgeonfish

Male
sea turtles
never leave the
ocean.

35

OCEAN Extremes

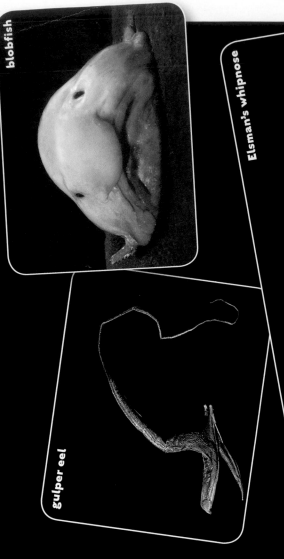

blobfish

gulper eel

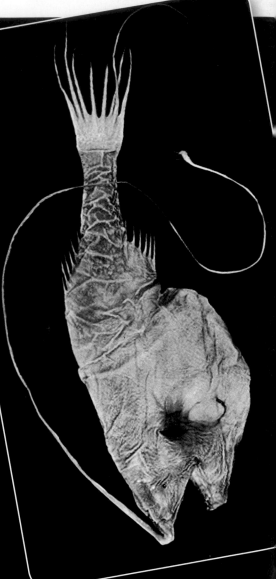

Elsman's whipnose

BIZARRE CREATURES OF THE DEEP

Pitch-black and just a few degrees above freezing, the ocean bottom is a harsh place to live, and the fish that survive in these extreme conditions have developed some strange adaptations. Most of these deep-sea residents are bioluminescent, which means chemicals inside their often see-through bodies glow like underwater night-lights. Sporting gargantuan mouths and spiky fangs, some have stretchy stomachs made for catching any meal that happens to fall their way.

barreleye fish

deep-sea anglerfish

hatchetfish

GULPER EEL

Depth: 1,640 to 24,600 feet (500 to 7,500 m)

Weird but True: Some gulper eels' mouths are bigger than their bodies.

BLOBFISH

Depth: 1,968 to 3,937 feet (600 to 1,200 m)

Weird but True: Instead of chasing prey, a blobfish may just open its oversize mouth and let food fall in.

ELSMAN'S WHIPNOSE

Depth: 0 to 16,400 feet (0 to 5,000 m)

Weird but True: Females can be 15 inches (40 cm) long; males are less than an inch (2.2 cm) long.

BARRELEYE FISH

Depth: 2,000 to 2,600 feet (610 to 792 m)

Weird but True: This fish has green, tube-shaped eyes and a see-through dome on its head.

DEEP-SEA ANGLERFISH

Depth: 2,600 to 5,280 feet (793 to 1,609 m)

Weird but True: The female has a glowing dorsal fin that acts as a fishing rod and lure.

HATCHETFISH

Depth: 1,310 to 4,130 feet (399 to 1,259 m)

Weird but True: It emits blue light that matches dim sunlight filtering through the water—a form of camouflage called counterillumination.

Dolphins **sleep** with **one** eye open.

DOLPHINS

SEVERAL QUICK TAIL PUMPS propel a shiny bottlenose dolphin through the water, leaping up into the air and then splashing headfirst into the ocean. Ultra-smooth skin, curved fins, and a streamlined body help the dolphin twirl gracefully through the air and slice through the water at speeds up to 14 miles an hour (23 kph).

Cruising along, the marine mammal surfaces every ten minutes or so to suck in air through its blowhole. Even taking a nap doesn't stop the dolphin—half of its brain always stays awake, telling the animal when to breathe.

These social marine mammals are some of the most advanced communicators in the sea. Squeaks, clicks, and chirps alert other dolphins in their group, or pod, to food or a predator lurking close by. They even send each other messages using body language, such as tail slaps and fin rubs.

Dolphins also use echolocation to "see" with their ears. Bouncing a series of clicks off of other animals or objects, the mammals then use the echoes to figure out how far away an object is and which way it is moving. Then whistle, click, whoosh. They're off again.

Atlantic bottlenose dolphin

MEET THE DOLPHINS

Dolphins and whales are closely related and belong to a group of marine mammals called cetaceans. So when is a dolphin a dolphin? Generally smaller than whales, dolphins often have narrower jaws and always have teeth. Many whales are toothless. Take a look at some of the coolest dolphins in the sea.

SPINNER
Length: 6 to 7 feet (1.8 to 2.1 m)
Weird but True: Some of the most acrobatic dolphins, they can twirl in the air four times in a row.

RISSO'S
Length: 8.5 to 13 feet (2 to 6.4 m)
Weird but True: These scrappy dolphins are covered with scars, often from roughhousing with other Risso's.

PACIFIC WHITE-SIDED
Length: 5 ½ to 8 feet (1.7 to 2.5 m)
Weird but True: Like many dolphins, Pacific white-sided dolphins like to play with seaweed.

ORCA
Length: 23 to 32 feet (8.2 to 9.6 m)
Weird but True: Often called "killer whales," orcas are actually the world's largest dolphins.

ATLANTIC SPOTTED
Length: 5 to 7.5 feet (1.6 to 2.3 m)
Weird but True: Atlantic spotted dolphins get more spots as they age.

spinner

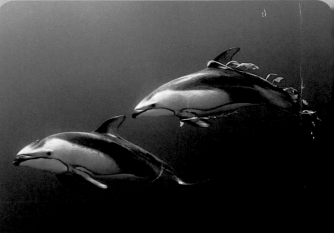
Pacific white-sided

Risso's

orca

Atlantic spotted

Dolphin "Speak"

BEHAVIOR	THE DOLPHIN MIGHT BE SAYING
Rubbing fins after being apart	Hello! I missed you.
S-shaped body posture	Watch out!
Approach from behind	Let's play!
Tail-slapping	Back off!
Touching fin to the side of another dolphin	Hey, give me a hand.

Coleman's shrimp

Shrimp **swim** backward.

CRUSTACEANS

SCUTTLING ALONG ON JOINTED LEGS, pincers constantly picking at the rocks and sand in a quest for food, crustaceans are built for self-protection. Popular snacks for sea otters, hammerhead sharks, and hundreds of other sea animals, some of these crawlers hide by digging holes in the squishy mud. But crabs, lobsters, shrimps, and other crustaceans carry their most important line of defense on their backs: hard shells, or carapaces, that make the animals difficult to swallow and challenging to chew.

As crustaceans grow, they molt, shedding their old shells and growing new ones that fit better. The swap happens as often as once a month for fast-growing young crustaceans, but the older they get, the longer their shells stay intact. For crabs, the new shells take a couple of days to harden, which makes them easy prey until their protection is back in place.

Many of these scavengers have antennae above their mouths and a pair of claws just below their mouths that they use to grab prey. Some crustaceans, such as lobsters, have larger claws on one side that come in handy for crushing shells, while the smaller claw is perfect for picking out the meat. Chomping everything from plants to other crustaceans to dead animals, crustaceans generally aren't picky about what they pinch.

spiny scallop

Mollusks

SCALLOPS, CLAMS, and oysters are familiar mollusks that might appear on the dinner table, but there are actually about 100,000 different species of mollusks. Ranging from smaller than an inch to more than 26 feet (8 m) long, some of these soft-bodied animals have shells, while others are shell free, such as octopuses and squid. Instead of molting like crustaceans, many mollusks keep building their shells for their entire lives. Small mollusks are fast food for predators such as sea stars, sea otters, crabs, and many other sea creatures.

Size: **9 to 10 feet (2.7 to 3.1 m)**

MANATEES

SOME EARLY EXPLORERS SPIED manatees with seaweed draped over their bodies and mistook them for mermaids. But in reality, these gentle giants look more like sumo wrestlers than mermaids. Sometimes called sea cows, full-grown manatees weigh in at a whopping 800 to 1,300 pounds (362 to 589 kg) and can eat as much as a tenth of their own weight in sea grasses and other plants every day.

Flicking their strong, paddle-shaped tails, manatees glide along at a leisurely five miles an hour (8 kph)—so slowly that algae can actually cling to their soft, wrinkly skin. But these marine mammals can ratchet up to 20 miles an hour (32 kph) when necessary. Living in warm, shallow waters, manatees use their front flippers to steer, sticking their lumpy snouts above the water's surface every 10 to 25 minutes to gulp air.

A mama manatee gives birth underwater and helps her baby to the surface for its first breath. Within minutes, the three-foot-long (91 cm) baby will start swimming but will stick with mom, nursing on her milk for the first year of its life.

A Manatee's Haven

MANGROVES ARE AN IDEAL REST STOP for manatees and a home to many other animals. A jumble of skinny roots and low-hanging branches, mangrove trees (below) thrive in estuaries, where freshwater and saltwater mix. Oysters and barnacles anchor themselves to the trees' dense roots, helping to filter water and trap nutrients in the woody stems. The result is a nutrient-packed nursery for young fish, sharks, crustaceans, and shellfish. Mangroves also provide nesting and hunting areas for seabirds. Keeping mangroves healthy is an important part of protecting ocean animals.

manatee in Florida, U.S.A.

The manatee's closest **relative** on **land** is the **elephant.**

OCEAN Extremes

Super Subs

Submersibles, or submarine-like diving machines, are built to withstand the massive pressure of the deep ocean. Scientists maneuver through the water, taking along lights, cameras, and recording equipment to help them document what they see. One of the most famous submersibles, called Alvin, can journey as deep as 4,764 feet (1,452 m) and has made more than 4,400 dives.

Alvin surfacing with ROV

Ice Buckets

A massive ship called an icebreaker crashes through the iceberg-filled polar waters. Slowing to a halt, the ship extends a crane-like arm that lowers explorers onto nearby ice in a people-size basket. Scientists examine the frozen terrain, gathering information from these dangerously cold and icy regions. Then the bucket lifts them to safety aboard the warm ship.

biologists in Antarctic ocean

Undersea Robots

Remotely Operated Vehicles, or ROVs (below), can journey as deep as 2,400 feet (731 m). A scientist on a ship uses a joystick to steer the robots to areas that are too dangerous for humans to go. Connected to ships with cables, ROVs have robotic arms that delicately pluck samples from the seafloor. This new generation of unmanned vehicles are helping to bring the mysteries of the sea to the surface.

Diver with ROV

Deepest Dive

This JIM suit—which controls pressure and temperature—helped oceanographer Sylvia Earle make the deepest ocean dive ever to 1,250 feet (381 m) below the surface (big image).

INTO THE UNKNOWN

Humans know more about the surface of the moon than they do about the bottom of the ocean. Like outer space, the ocean is an unfriendly environment for human survival. The deeper you travel, the more intense the water pressure becomes. Without protection, human skulls and bones would be crushed, and veins and arteries would collapse. Plus, extremely cold temperatures (above and below the surface) could be life-threatening. These extreme machines help scientists stay safe while they explore the secret world beneath the waves.

Male marine iguanas **butt heads** for up to **five** hours when **battling** over females.

marine iguana swimming

MARINE IGUANAS

SWISHING FROM SIDE TO SIDE, flat tail floating behind, the marine iguana swims through tropical waters and tidal pools. It is the only sea-going lizard on the planet.

Coming ashore for a rest or a good meal, the lizards use their long, sharp claws to grab on tight to rocks as they munch seaweed and scrape algae off the rocks with their sharp teeth. When food is scarce for months, marine iguanas not only get skinnier but also shorter. The animal's spine actually shrinks and then expands again when the animal can find more seaweed treats.

Life as an air-breathing reptile that feeds in the water has its drawbacks. Every few minutes or so, a marine iguana's bulbous, rock-like snout shoots above the surface to suck in air. This creature can swallow a lot of salt water with its algae meals, because a special gland near its eyes collects the salt that its body doesn't need. When the prehistoric-looking lizard is back on land, *aaaa-choooo!* It sneezes out the salty stuff in a burst of tiny flakes. Drifting down like snow, the flakes cling to its bumpy head like a funny-looking white wig.

The Galápagos Islands

STRONG OCEAN CURRENTS SWIRL around the Galápagos islands, off the coast of Ecuador, South America. On the shores, tidal pools sit at the feet of volcanic rock and rough boulders. Chilly waters surround the entire archipelago.

Straddling the Equator, the Galápagos (both pictures) are home to animals found nowhere else in the world, including marine iguanas, giant tortoises that can live to be more than a hundred years old, and flightless cormorants, some of the rarest birds in the world.

49

WALRUSES

SNOUT DOWN IN THE SANDY SEAFLOOR,

a walrus sweeps its face back and forth, using its whiskers to scrounge for clams. In seconds, the walrus swallows one down and spits out the shell. The giants polish off dozens of pounds of the shellfish every day to keep their 3,700-pound (1,678-kg) bodies moving through the ocean.

When the walrus is done with its underwater feast, the animal swishes its tail to push its massive body up through water. Face poking through the surface for a breath, the walrus spurts water to clean out its fishy-smelling whiskers.

Using its three-foot-long tusks to haul itself onto the ice for a rest, a walrus rotates its strong flippers under its body and then raises its body up for a look around. But the animal is anything but graceful when it walks on land, clumsily flopping along like a gigantic inchworm.

Walruses spend most of their time feeding in the water, following the sea ice north as it melts in the summer, and then heading south again in the winter as the ice returns. Staying warm is a team effort for these social animals. Hundreds of walruses pile up, their blubbery bodies keeping each other cozy.

Seals (including sea lions) and walruses make up a family of marine mammals called pinnipeds, which have flipperlike limbs. Find out some of the differences between sea lions and their walrus relatives.

SEA LION vs. WALRUS

SEA LION	WALRUS
do not have tusks	have tusks
front flippers propel them through water	hind flippers propel them through water; front flippers steer
have ear flaps on the outside	have internal ears
have 40 to 60 whiskers	have 400 to 700 whiskers
up to 11 feet (3.3 m) long	up to 12 feet (3.7 m) long

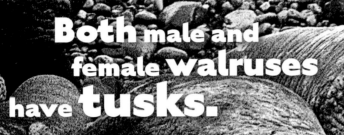

Both male and female **walruses** have **tusks.**

walruses hauled
out on a beach

A great white shark
can **weigh** as
much as **ten gorillas.**

great white shark off
the coast of Mexico

A GREAT WHITE SHARK detects splashing up near the ocean's surface. Getting a swimming start, the powerful predator smashes through the surface, grabbing a desperately flapping seal. Then, flipping head over tail, the shark slams against the water again. Great whites never even chew their bites. Instead, the shark rips the seal into chunks. It can swallow smaller prey whole.

Sleek and silent, sharks prowl through the watery depths, stalking fish, seals, squid, and other sea creatures. In the eat-or-be-eaten world of the ocean, sharks almost always come out on top. With

SHARKS

sharp vision, muscular bodies, and the ability to smell blood from a distance, great whites are designed to hunt. Before a shark even sees a fish, it can detect the animal's heartbeat with electric sensory preceptors. These tiny, gel-filled canals in the shark's snout, called the ampullae of Lorenzini, let the hunter know when prey may be hiding nearby.

With skin that's designed to reduce the water's drag on the body, this sleek predator speeds through the water. Some sharks can cruise up to 20 miles (32 km) an hour. Once these stealthy predators have settled on their supper, escape doesn't come easy.

FACE-TO-FACE WITH SHARKS

The top of the food chain and the biggest fish in the sea, a shark's job is to weed out weak members of other species to prevent overpopulation. Sharks may seem scary, but they often get a bad rap. Only about four fatal shark attacks on humans occur each year; humans are actually a much greater threat to sharks. Get up close and personal with some of these powerful predators.

LONGNOSE SAWSHARK
Length: up to 5 feet (1.5 m)
Weird but True: The teeth of a baby longnose sawshark are folded back until it's born so it doesn't scratch its mom's body.

LEMON SHARK
Length: 8 to 10 feet (2.4 to 3 m)
Weird but True: When flipped onto their backs, lemon shark babies become naturally paralyzed for several minutes—a state called tonic immobility.

HAMMERHEAD SHARK
Length: 6 to 14 feet (1.8 to 4.2 m)
Weird but True: A hammerhead gives birth to live babies called pups.

NURSE SHARK
Length: 7.5 to 9 feet (2.3 to 2.7 m)
Weird but True: Nurse sharks use suction to slurp prey off the seafloor.

WHALE SHARK
Length: up to 40 feet long (12 m)
Weird but True: Each whale shark has a unique pattern of spots, like a human fingerprint.

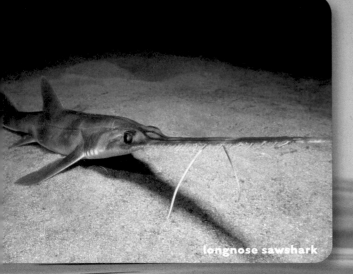

longnose sawshark

hammerhead shark

lemon shark

nurse shark

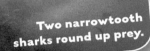

Two narrowtooth sharks round up prey.

Who
EATS WHOM

PREDATOR	PREY
great white	mostly seals, sea lions, and fish
tiger shark	anything, including other sharks
whale shark	mostly plankton, some squid and fish
hammerhead, nurse, longnose sawshark	crabs, shrimp squid, and other sea life

20 WAYS YOU CAN PROTECT THE OCEAN

You can make a big difference when it comes to protecting the planet. These 20 tips help conserve water, keep pollution out of oceans, and protect the animals that live there. Be blue to be green!

1. Get moving. Bike or walk as much as possible to keep car oil and other chemicals from running off into waterways.

2. Don't release pets such as fish or snakes into rivers, lakes, or the ocean. Non-native animals can harm the ecosystem.

3. Participate in a beach cleanup.

4. Be a water monitor. Report leaks and drips at home and at school.

5. Take short showers instead of baths. Set a timer to see how clean you can get in five minutes.

6. Never release helium balloons into the air. When they fall into the water, animals can mistake them for food.

7. Make your own soap out of leftover soap slivers to keep pieces of soap from going down the drain—and possibly into waterways. Squish the slivers into cool shapes when they're wet.

8. Avoid using the toilet as a trash can. Flushing things such as medicine may contaminate water sources. It also wastes water.

9. Scoop the poop! Keep your pet's business from ending up in water sources.

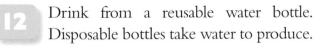
Adélie penguin

10 When your family stays at a hotel, reuse towels, washcloths, and sheets.

11 Paint "no dumping" art on storm drains (with nontoxic paint) by joining a stenciling program with your town or city. This encourages people to keep paint, trash, and soapy water from car washes out of storm drains, which often flows into lakes, rivers, and oceans.

12 Drink from a reusable water bottle. Disposable bottles take water to produce.

13 Water your lawn or garden in the early morning. Water doesn't evaporate as fast when the air is cool, so you won't need as much.

14 Recycle so your trash doesn't end up in water sources.

15 Volunteer at a local aquarium to learn about ocean animals and conservation.

16 Scrape leftovers into the trash instead of rinsing them down the disposal, or make compost.

17 Keep your dog on a leash at the beach. Loose dogs can scare or harm creatures that live there.

18 Water is used to produce just about everything, so buy only what you need.

19 Don't feed water animals. They need to find their own food to keep themselves—and their environment—healthy.

20 Share these blue tips with friends and family.

LAYERS OF LIFE

At the ocean's greatest depths, the seafloor is almost seven miles (11 km) below the water's surface. Under the waves, even in places where the sun never shines, beautiful and strange life-forms find ways to thrive.

SUNLIGHT ZONE

From the ocean's surface to about 328 feet (100 m) below the waves, plants, plankton, and animals soak up the abundant sunlight filtering through the waves. Sea creatures big and small feast in this nourishing underwater garden.

TWILIGHT ZONE

Very little sunlight reaches the twilight zone, between about 328 (100 m) and 3,300 feet (1,006 m) deep. No plants can survive here. Only a few kinds of living things flourish this deep, such as jellyfish and bacteria. Fish, squid, and shrimp travel between the sunlight and twilight zones in search of food. And sperm whales search for squid at this level in hopes of scoring a tasty meal. But these animals return to the sunlight zone before long.

MIDNIGHT ZONE

Dropping from roughly 3,300 feet (1,006 m) to the ocean's deepest trench, almost 36,000 feet (10,973 m) down, the midnight zone encompasses some three-quarters of the ocean, where the temperature hovers near a frigid 39°F (4°C) and light rays fade away. To survive, deep-sea creatures have adapted strange ways to hunt and scavenge (see pages 36–37).

1. blue shark
2. common dolphin
3. yellow sea horse
4. bluegirdled angelfish
5. clown triggerfish
6. moonfish
7. flyingfish
8. green sea turtle
9. comb jellyfish
10. sunfish
11. Portuguese man-of-war
12. humpback whale
13. harbor porpoise
14. common eagle ray
15. jellyfish
16. bluefin tuna
17. Pacific giant octopus
18. plankton
19. deep-sea squid
20. viperfish
21. lanternfish
22. deep-sea glass squid
23. bell jelly
24. hatchetfish
25. sperm whale
26. dragonfish
27. giant squid
28. rattail fish
29. deep-sea zooplankton
30. snipe eel
31. vampire octopus
32. siphonophore
33. black seadevil
34. black swallower
35. antimora
36. smoothhead
37. anglerfish
38. gulper eel
39. fangtooth
40. amphipod
41. crown jellyfish
42. decapod
43. barreleye fish
44. deep-sea zooplankton
45. tripodfish
46. giant sea spider
47. glass sponge
48. snailfish
49. deep-sea cucumber
50. brittle star

ILLUSTRATION NOT TO SCALE

SUNLIGHT

TWILIGHT

MIDNIGHT

GLOSSARY

adapt—to change in order to increase the chances of surviving in a specific environment

Antarctic—the region around the continent of Antarctica

Arctic—the region north of the Arctic Circle

bacteria—tiny, one-celled organisms found in plants, soil, water, air, and animals' bodies

baleen—a hard, comblike material that grows in the upper jaws of baleen whales and is used for filtering plankton from water

bioluminescence—light chemically produced by a living creature

blowhole—a nostril on the top of the head of a cetacean, which is a scientific name for marine mammals like whales and dolphins

camouflage—colors or patterns on an animal's body that help it blend in with its surroundings

carnivore—an animal that eats other animals

cephalopods—a group of marine mollusks, including squid and octopuses, that have several arms, suckers on their arms, and squirt ink for self-defense

cetaceans—a group of marine mammals, including whales and dolphins

coral reef—a rocky ridge of coral shells built up over years as the coral animals inside die

crustacean—an animal with a hard, outer shell, joined body, and legs that lives in water, such as a crab, lobster, or shrimp

current—a distinct stream of water that flows within an ocean

cyclone feeding—a process of feeding where manta rays circle around and around

food chain—the order in which one organism eats another in an ecosystem

hydrothermal vents—areas in the seafloor where magma-heated water shoots up into the freezing-cold seawater around it

iceberg—a drifting mass of ice broken off from an ice sheet or glacier

jet propulsion—when an animal, such as a squid or octopus, squirts a jet of water from its body to propel the animal forward

kelp—a type of seaweed that grows extremely tall in coastal waters

krill—a tiny, shrimplike creature that forms the basis of the diet of baleen whales

magma—molten rock under Earth's crust

mammals—warm-blooded animals that breathe air, usually give birth to live young, have fur or hair, and nurse their young

marine—of or relating to the ocean

Mariana Trench—a long, narrow valley in the Pacific Ocean that contains the deepest point in the ocean, some 35,827 feet (10,972 m) under the surface

Mid-Atlantic Ridge—a 6,214-mile-long (10,000 km) mountain range under the ocean

midnight zone—the layer of the ocean from 3,300 feet (1,006 m) down to the bottom of the ocean, where there is no sunlight

mollusks—a group of soft-bodied animals that lack backbones, are not divided into segments, and are sometimes covered in hard shells, such as clams, mussels, and oysters

plankton—tiny plants and animals that are food for many ocean animals

pinniped—a marine mammal, such as a walrus, seal, or sea lion, that has four flippers as limbs

polyp—a coral or sea anemone that has a mouth surrounded by tentacles

predator—an animal that hunts or kills another animal for food

prey—an animal that is hunted or killed by another animal for food

ROV (Remotely Operated Vehicle)—an unmanned, underwater vehicle for ocean exploration that humans operate by remote control

scavenge—to feed on dead animals

submersible—a manned underwater vehicle used for ocean exploration that is built to travel to great depths

sunlight zone—the layer of the ocean from the surface to 328 feet (100 m), where there is abundant sunlight

tentacle—a long, flexible extension, usually on the head or mouth of an animal, used by the animal to touch or grab

twilight zone—the layer of the ocean from 328 (100 m) to 3,300 feet (1,006 m) deep, where there is little sunlight

venom—poison transmitted to other animals by biting or stinging

Boldface indicates illustrations.

PUBLISHED BY THE NATIONAL GEOGRAPHIC SOCIETY

John M. Fahey, Jr., *President and Chief Executive Officer*
Gilbert M. Grosvenor, *Chairman of the Board*
Tim T. Kelly, *President, Global Media Group*
John Q. Griffin, *President, Publishing*
Nina D. Hoffman, *Executive Vice President; President, Book Publishing Group*
Melina Gerosa Bellows, *Executive Vice President, Children's Publishing*

PREPARED BY THE BOOK DIVISION

Nancy Laties Feresten, *Vice President, Editor in Chief, Children's Books;* Jonathan Halling, *Design Director, Children's Publishing;* Jennifer Emmett, *Executive Editor, Children's Books;* Carl Mehler, *Director of Maps;* R. Gary Colbert, *Production Director;* Jennifer A. Thornton, *Managing Editor*

STAFF FOR THIS BOOK

Robin Terry, *Project Editor;* James Hiscott, Jr., *Art Director;* Lori Epstein, *Illustrations Editor;* Miriam Stein, *Photo and Digital Imaging Editor;* Wanda Jones, Ph.D., *Researcher;* Grace Hill, *Associate Managing Editor;* Heidi Vincent, *Vice President Direct Response Sales and Marketing;* Jeff Reynolds, *Marketing Director, Children's Books;* Lewis R. Bassford, *Production Manager;* Susan Borke, *Legal and Business Affairs*

MANUFACTURING AND QUALITY MANAGEMENT

Christopher A. Liedel, *Chief Financial Officer;* Phillip L. Schlosser, *Vice President;* Chris Brown, *Technical Director;* Rachel Faulise, *Manufacturing Manager;* Nicole Elliot, *Manufacturing Manager*

National Geographic's net proceeds support vital exploration, conservation, research, and education programs.

For more information, please call 1-800-NGS LINE (647-5463) or write to the following address:
National Geographic Society
1145 17th Street N.W.
Washington, D.C. 20036-4688 U.S.A.

Visit us online at nationalgeographic.com/books
For librarians and teachers: ngchildrensbooks.org
More for kids from National Geographic: kids.nationalgeographic.com

For information about special discounts for bulk purchases, please contact National Geographic Books Special Sales: ngspecsales@ngs.org

For rights or permissions inquiries, please contact National Geographic Books Subsidiary Rights: ngbookrights@ngs.org